B JENKINS

REFIGURING
AMERICAN MUSIC
A series edited by
Ronald Radano and Josh Kun
Charles McGovern,
contributing editor

B Jenkins

FRED MOTEN

DUKE
UNIVERSITY
PRESS
Durham & London 2010

© 2010 Duke University Press
All rights reserved
Printed in the United States of America
on acid-free paper ∞
Designed by Jennifer Hill
Typeset in Minion Pro
by Tseng Information Systems, Inc.
Library of Congress Cataloging-in-
Publication Data appear on the
last printed page of this book.

The interview printed at the end of this book originally
appeared as "Words Don't Go There: An Interview with
Fred Moten," *Callaloo* 27, no. 4 (2004): 953–66.

Versions of some of the following poems have
appeared in these magazines: *Callaloo, Can We Have
Our Ball Back?, Chain, Five Fingers Review, Hambone,
Lift, Masthead, nocturnes, PO-EP, The Poetry Project
Newsletter, Shuffleboil, Small Press Traffic, The World.*
In addition, some versions appeared in Jim Behrle and
Fred Moten, *Poems* (Pressed Wafer, 2002).

for zozo and chili

contents

b jenkins

b jenkins

Her territory sunflower, insurgent floor time in real time in the field
museum—bertha lee and her lyric ways and her urban plan. up and down
the regular highway and every two-tone station, passing through
to cure, for preservation to unfold it all away, she put the new thing
in the open cell, one more time about the theory of who we are.

> In the names away in blocks
> with double names to interrupt and
> gather, kept dancing in tight circles
> between break and secret, vaulted
> with records in our basement, where
> the long-haired hippies and afro-
> blacks all get together across the
> tracks and they party, everybody sown
> like grain and touched in stride.

> Now the cold new reckoning is tired and you've been
> waiting for a preferential song. the multiplex should be in the
> frame like bodies in a house way back in the woods, fled in
> suspended projects like the real thing, posed for the midnight
> trill. essential shtetl of the world stage, born way before you
> was born, move the administered word by breathing, to hand
> beautiful edge around.

gayl jones

my daddy drank red soda pop.
once he wanted a fleetwood,
then he wanted a navigator,
so he could navigate, check out

his radio towers, deliver flowers,
drive back to give me long kisses,

watch mama burn her books. said nancy

wilson can't sing but she can style—
hold back the force of random operators/
return to the line refuse to punctuate. a moon—
but his actual drive was watching clay circle,

tight-breath'd hunch, tight shoulder. sweet

nancy wilson was just cold analytics:

the difference between a new coat and the
one with ink on the pocket, calculate

like a fat young minister, strokin' like

clarence carter, increase like creflo
dollar. mama and me stayed up over

the club, cried sometimes in the same
broke off the same piece left each other

the last piece practiced the same piece
got warm on the same. however,
I'm so full this morning I have
to try and make you understand

billie holiday

grain, you changed on the hill past
baker, grain of sand, ignored every
star, folded every grain seared

to any other voice once knew.
never any other voice once knew just
seared to darken lavender to night

of the old new ooh ooh and the old

new moon, wait a while, piercing
through, her seizure closes, after an

own aunt of mine, a triptych

before the break like clear satin,
microphone grain, fitted whisper
like a crack and pin. in satin on fifteen

rough edge surround me. you're
breaking my heart. like clear satin
thick water streamed out your

mouth. the pitch of your transfer

went from way up high. a man
held your air in his hands till
bright condensation ripped

your voice back to the desert air
before the broken fruit stand,

it's a little alone, it's a little alone,

the echo anticipate, the hard
bloom underbreath, the album
eruption. urge graphics bend grain

and strife come turn the grain again
grain, fifteen grain, her long secret road
of hiding, surge and observation

roland barthes

wanda jean allen

who was gene talking to
if she wasn't talking to
the ones who were enjoying

her abjection and the prospect
of her death and her death?

the fourth and fifth fifths of
oklahoma the video refusal
the open thing partially
the strife enjoy the I'm
'on' kill something the rasp and

destiny of the servant girl the

c-melody the trusted one
the disavow and holiday
and execute the disavow apologize
the whispering objection

kendall thomas

jeanne moreau

refuse the elevator to
the falsify, arise arise.

refuse the brand new scar

and whole to mute the homily.

close and track
(hold and send, hold and send
I lost you
I love you, it's a little alone

wave river wave savannah
leave. arise between the wall
and held. sent to

refuse arise

miles davis

charlie jenkins

for phase till one was left

to let the others know. pass
the underground song by

hebron curve, ghost apron,
haze but look ayonder

keeping on. the last crop
was rich and thin. that big

but he was always just that
small. lean miles against the
wheel till one and here I am

for elegy and underground,
stride and suffer, spiced
peaches, almost bent
too far for one last

strut, the protest
and arrive.

james brown

or start with d end

Aguszda Diaz.

this is a social art to get the
sound of the voice in writing.

art of social development and phrase
abstraction. relation to social reality

is higher than any realism. but the
sentence is an abstraction. so there

are two, deformations, extensions,

fragmentations and augmentations

leading up to the twist and crusha

these minimum standards in flame

as if*ah hhh (and thrust in big revolution, hidden drum
unhhch*un) for a treatise on the politics of sound

henry dumas

new air in marianna is aloft

                               in mountain home. like ra

the form is visible   but it comes back curved
        but not eroded

                                  in the leaning air.
                                    soft in helena

terrible in sweet home

                         like a pearl   but faded black.

fishbone

the fucked up globe
desegregation

band. fold sweet

bird cold be free

bass world new
ground jailed
eights, world's set. broke

in small fly packs,

change the move
make deep come back,

trace a pattern on the edge, a crack
in universal city's magic fade

along the track,

black paladin, off and out to school.

the holy sphere
experimental

band

joseph jarman

elvin jones, malachi favors, steve lacy

on the one hand the right hand
that the left hand
is fluted. on the other hand

I give away my hand,

advance in touches,
but she slowly in her
shawl, half-flute
full shell).

stretched polyphone, the el on division
continuing the city for an ell

(thin line,
yellow shimmers, thin line, evidence and cherry

alexander weheliye, lygia clark, ed roberson

the chance became a method.

songspeak and the folded animals

and the penetrated exile. tropical

devotion in the form of deviant
scholarship. the form for disturbing

flowers shhhhh. lean to the secret whole
in buildings. lena's airshaft. loss's party!

sherrie tucker, francis ponge, sun ra

where the universal
girl from magic
city, the pre-holiday
gardenia,

cultural student

of perfect image

perfect meadow?

Please wait.

pantomime daughters
shriek inside out
overdub,
scar, swing
before trumpet,
flute, fade

half-flute
harfleur and cherry

gary fisher

[1]

me and rodvan went for doubles and doubles.
rodvan took me for doubles and doubles.
doubles and doubles and doubles and doubles in alleys.

told me a story bout him and his boys eating doubles and doubles.

the alley was for beatings. excess invasions and secret tents,
long puppets and wild meat. doubles and doubles of secret passage

and doubles without accident. doubles and beatings and accidental
revenue. dance all night in the basement for secret meetings. hold out
your hand with gifts and open secret greetings. innings and innings and
doubles and doubles and doubles. small sharp spice and paste of chick

pea, roti plump like the palm of my hand, doubles and doubles of

underground carolina. gather the ones who are looking for nothing but
trouble in the new colonial office, everything stained with love and hate
for the flavor of repeating. doubles and doubles and doubles.

[2]

people saying always already known reality and
sometimes it's *that* you say some shit. this is
Gary's performance Gary in the music too

Gary on the scene and in the scene. Gary Fisher
want you to be attached to this pocket totality
and essence Gary Prince Gary Jacobs. blow the
last autobiography of secrecy and reticence

more wild than beloved with fever and grasping

how he looked at this. can you? can't you?

beautiful coming and going and passionate bind
(on the one hand judy on the other hand), eve,
my injury is always behind me singing prove
it on me midnight sun, stomp, sugar,

shoo bee doo bee I want to be free

[3]

how long you wait for everything is you.
I fill the pitcher up. I sing in boxes.)
me and Gary moved into the house you left

and never saw each other again. Rodvan

started jacking people up on the corner,

syncopation like a housekeeper, welcoming. meanwhile
I'm packing this bullshit up. on the other hand
I think I'll make me a world. broke off the wide
way up to the eloquence of gesture let your

head turn, let your blush spread. but other than
the barbarism of reading your own shame, sing, too,
while we just laugh and come and laugh and run
because we too baroque to pay attention

yopie prins

teddie
hates that
he loves jazz

and loves that.
june steals breath

from breathing, totes

air from tables, bangs
by singing, friends

with posing, oboes
the burdened

palisade.

robert farris thompson

why everything got to mean something?
you can too make up

the real thing

which ain't nothing like
no letter, nothing fresh
in the mind like a model,
but the 'leventh eye
like a reprograph

reprobate ethnograph
seen nine times, twelve

times, move me, groove me

like John Taggart.

but your suit and stance are

most too fresh as every atom
making up the real like that
in slipped penetration nouveau

hear this afro afro afro music

listen to some of this super black music
welcome, philosophy!

brent edwards

                    as
cleanhead vinson as bob
o'meally, thorough dome.

complaint, with threads

then braid through grain (pump up
the jam. break the jam. theory of the jam
is brent edwards. of the mix before. the spray of the

cross long echo. the mute and dream
of all the time but off the track)

and contrabass. grave
sandals free alphabet

carafe d'eau alphaville drone accent

grave. restrain blue that queen mab

(but kidd glove (oakland guards) or betty switch
induce my friend's bright twitch!

bessie smith

seance   open-lid eyes

called back a long time longed long   long

driven hold for a redelivery
and giving you back what you keep—

                    or a parable or
romance   photographer unidentified

give breath John's gala brightness of James
through the snow of another village or strange

on the other hand your shit comes so heavy satin shadow for

            song

for   circle for long longed
up under two perfumes, hair shines so shows shone
so that it comes so hard on you pierce so blunt that you

off to the side for and turn smile long long say

she move through the black velvet curtain

jean-michel basquiat

so people would notice em

M

        crown

I just made that crossing out air myself. thank you
    ohhh but not that mood

               there © zhagged with accent sans
teeth   jagged

    atmettiene

    time is now

never heard so much pretty music before like that. I was surprised and
filled. you know it's got to be new york that makes you question all that

noise and tires, baskets, pallets. all about what it means to slip in boxes

what they move early at the docks boatloads and docks and fucked-up
carfulls. now whenever I see her bounce/arm bend more free time. did

you have shoes on in that VanDerZee portrait? there. M and crown.

track of bricks. vixtory

alice key

[ENTER THE SCENE]

the short stairs from room

to room the increments of
groups

      some people walking

and a hand touches somebody's

event, somebody's coat. step down rise behind that yellow

sweater fadelike song. this a
gallery of octagons and the band's
a train of steps up open windows
frames wide matting and low running

maybe the edge of the water. the half grand

up ahead, in the street I started,

before your used to be, open door, unclean
corners, lab,
labyrinth of manchester, andy
kirk, andy cole, chanting, canton, noon to noon

[TO THE AFTERPARTY]

the framed-up trip of her name
the afterparty. I gotta make a call.

it's a little alone, it's a little alone,

this ain't my edge, this inside edge.
I'm on the massed up rack of these sound events
like edward, posing in your bathtub, holds the shaft
with an ear for painting, one fold, auburn rough

mobile and object through well formed: a moon
mobile and object through well formed: a mood

james baldwin

hey somebody, some jewels lined up
like hard flowers. pull that one

jump the hidden balcony the air

get pierced and snared
and soft down to the street and roll
to Fanelli's. the booming walk of goods
all over the buckled street like Fred

Hopkins. towers peeking over the corner

of temples. somebody's window is

covered by a book with pictures.

hollow circle and round edge scream
and shatter the material. a whole buncha
ribbons like a choir.

                          you can walk
through the bookshelf to a bloody corner:
pull foner and that late wagon creak

to the next dockery. a little dug out

cave out there in the broughton settlement.

the bow of a fiddle and broke tea cup.
a quilt made of grass and big ol' legs
'sleep in the other room. they shot her

twenty-three times and hit her twelve.
woke up when her back collapsed but
that's all over now. the white on black like

glare ride the chute the old-new city: mama

and Ms. Key an 'nem whispering.

if the phone ring

somebody's plan and stall that cut pause

distended horn recall. this is the end

of the open passage: sullivan, tunapuna,
that late night pan and worker's
party, the logical jam of their future

in my present of not only his bridge

but these other bridges too, the band
spread out into the audience, the cook sitting
at your table, a little hard beauty's swallowing

eyes, home through the sharp rapidness of some notes.

william parker

my town is very large array. look at me
look up inside my circle and my sounds at

my music to my left at the birds in the tree

machine. my music dreams about my mama to

my boy. they sing to each other in a secret

for the ordinary culture, the folded play

on the street about bird pretending and flute
stealing till it's time to go to play mountain.

all this is in the nature of my shelves.
they are the head archive of very large array

and if you listen close birmingham and the

wind blowin' in from chicago, throwin' ends
from chicago, california and rossville, tennessee

and hamtramck, michigan to united sound

are all together on the longest road I know

cut door by door in violent courtyards.

they decided their skirts meant something
to do with movement in the page frame, song

for a moving picture of the tone world, for

the remote trio, the internal world theater,

inner ear of the inside songs, the inside

songs of curtis mayfield by william parker,

theater in the near, flavor that inside
outside opening, the ear's folds, its courses,

in the open space, do it to me in my common

ear hole, its porches, insurge of the tone will,

gone in the sound booth, deep in da inner

sound ya'll, invasive song up in you to get down

through everybody's open window. now
my broke inside is a tent city. I live hard

in tent cities. my town is very large array

fred mcdowell

cecil taylor

klang and cut through
burning, texture,

but it's all basic

ornament and thread

too. through broken anaclitic feel

and long long cut and long

long reserve and long

the outstretched address three!

their incline song screams

bell and shaft and cant inside
the furnished discipline,

to polish the wooden

practice box, sometimes

dance, shake your arm
and move your form.

alamillo bears striving with
mysterious title and broken

law. in the colored water

cable stays on the scene as
sculpted numbers whirling

furniture and instrument

in and out of tone until

the leaning bridge says bye

mama. this also touches on

leaving just before moses cut

new york with express barrier

circles busting blocks. remember,

striving is aleatory for

beautiful black queens.

they end in open systems
as bridges given hour by hour.

almeida ragland

tony oxley

in baltimore then dive your brush
she sighs. cut thing, electric
shirt faded with cleaning,

beat between stones, ride!

indent along her side and brush
her cheek and broken collar her pad

below her curve and on her hair

rub some of that yellow salve.

        dessalines at putney in the pulse track

        from the ditch. over maximum
        independence to new model

        translate to cut the original
        shadow cozy cholly jo your hands.

        these hands are thirteen tones
of buried life. tone tone hold

the frenzied sun.

indented servant, all up in that squalled report run on

to the next stop all up in that gone

report run on. of many heads of sheffield denton

steel united inner
harbor frozen service

porch broken floor boards. fell loop, you paint

broken crop with mallet tangent tongues surge

service blush, presence wrapt in short
withdrawals in satin, barbed
with waiting, like a woman or a drum

frederick douglass

walter benjamin

is fear of intricate weaving on a table playing body and soul with john searle who's background transcribing a head arrangement. funhouse implicature, the city is a passage through the woods, hard row. on the track of things in fragments like a polish logician. shall we dance we will is shall we will a borderland. I'm a philosophical grammarian, reading

knots, playing taps, rolling, chanting curving in the evening when the

sun go down, 'cause my optical

circle for scarring is the black sun, canting pilgrimage and fellowship and missionary work of picking peas of john brazil, hard row. black and red was a pillar of salt and black and brown rage against empire. hosea hudson curled beside laboring women and black hunger. black rice and black fire from the city scrawlspace to the pyramids hinged on

collection, under distancing, so I'm living on that music again. the picture book is a word book

on that music again. I went to see if I could try to make her happy but I just chant blue and brown effect like that silk cress cecilia wore with her small voice in the black sun. I owe you the truth in stealing and I'll

sell it to you, holding petals and blue and brown strings and cut grass.

my friends are black like a country, move in the game like strangers,

break codes in the street, get loud on sundays in the streets, revive and drink some, gamble and huff.

julian boyd

peck curtis

little more edge selfrising all

that edge and rim. some other time

you could walk the bridge tonight
brush helena lula tap soft. that

water hit and wash light off the ground
every now and then. step   wait   there
free accident. cakes and pies. low
tremor underneath a squall on the corner
on a crate behind a toy kit. lever of the trap

door of the trap set hinge turn

release at the sidewalk crack slide

to the levee all the way down to
the bottom. the bottom of the ocean.
selfrising of this fall booms, g.

john thompson

like a blacksmith
the all blacks are

not any more than
all other things are
the man who wear

his blackness well

over his shoulder
like a towel.

one high fist is press
+ essence, michael

graham and patrick

back, the cold frenzy

up front like ahmad

jamal. jonah lomu's

edge and curve of black

block move like tony
smith (saginaw, michigan)
like dimitri chandler's
sculptural sister and
played with love like
gene smith like fierce

mourning open to some

one's loss and someone's

gift and all up in smith's

chest (whose name is a

locked set of jonahs
on eakins' contact
sheet like renee gladman
said) like smith was kyle
macy like he was the
new thing the sncc
barrelhouse played fire

soft like sonny murray's

moses blown inside and

down the black hand

side of the left hand
sideline. like a gem

hadar tufted booblehead

in a johnny cash black

and off-black onesie and
all black derby like sonny

boy williamson in helena
smuggling harp like trane
like sonny on the bridge
like black night falling

like michael graham

on sonny's time

now like peck curtis like
little brother montgomery
black-blocking art chords

slowly curling out the
blocks of new color like
tony smith singing
broken lines then sleek

burning flying breaking

windows in exile like
piet mondrian at fred

oakley's keen-toed

angled one high fist and
black-ribbed dress socks

curling straight out the

blocks in bright half-

diamonds like tommie

smith like john thompson's
high blacksmith hands
like nora nicolini

george gervin

at another dinner party

                              for these streets

                                               on east six seven

          they put a hoodie on

                              some timberlands

                                                    and a black

smith cube. chill, though.

                                        pick some ice in your

                            glass

               hold the snowflake. hesitate

                                                  and

afterthought. soon, a spur in your ass

                      otherwise

the mirror broke off
be comin atcha

michael fried

adrian piper

is for aural glancing. flowers
for albert carroll. come sunday
the object come back. I play

revolted midnights always

coming back. why they

always coming back, why they don't

stay down? this is the arché-object.

this is the modular shit. this the
real junk this the real funk

josé muñoz

"I love my students (why
         is this a performative?   I am I do what
                                          ever I say I do I am if I
                                                    wasn't then the full
                                          failure, flowers
                                          of barrel, of plenty flavor, the
                          curve of

                                                    my tongue

in their mouths

         because we let we leave.

              when everybody cries

in the face of an open work, the circle
         workshop, the transverse band
                          the broke-ass institute   the chaste
                 underground

                                          symposium of eve, bully, coco
call 'se'steban like a father, chicken and rice down low—

                                                    love can
bust you up in increments so

                                          you link ephemera
                                 substitute beautify

michael hanchard

don't cohere, they jam

a broken axe. but that's
up in my works and mess.

animéd bidness her

café her foe his breath

my city tunestress won't come here

on certainty's cool
relaxing harness.

                              the multiply
mess means set   organized constraint

        party   of the set is

cookable bunch   inoperative

    castor, cantor   as the

        stuff—my thing

                                                life of the party
my skills

    my shit, the shit

        I never knew you

        I never knew you
        had such pretty hair,

        the unelected corner
        said, for the love of

        turning, in the shadow

        of kermess. the unelected
        corner breathed in

modern blackness, the spare

luxurious spray of the
thirteenth commune, afro

black's black accent's

open luminescence of the
open road's black dust.

(the price is the name

of the house party,

flown all over
hobo and severe.

bad as it was for pretty boy,

right as how ya'll broke
against the tragic deputy,

can't buy the spray, and stole

some flowers, and stole away

and can't afford, the runaway

ran on my running board
and through my diatone.

                the priceless diatrane

is nicolo, the afrospur,

de rore's rerum, and my
kids to sing your name.

woody guthrie

thelma foote

you are my little fade

razor. your form delights

itself in disregard that passes
over you like heavy air
until you cut it back,

the heavy air that brings

economies of swale with

accident, my little trust maker.

groove against concrete
in your shallow depression,
and every little lovely thing,

nut brown, to lift you up

in prayer, just to reveal that

every limit is so high above,
every little thing in love made
air. oh wouldn't it be loverly

on aloes eve with minshalling

waves of string-curved wood

and steel swayed with cool

water from sliced rock to the
corner auto-dance, of the old

man trapcode, quadratic hips

and hand, to savor the alternate
mode inside! (your) form is fête

with just a little taper made

return and turn the long soft,
but also to enjoy percussion

in a brutal exercise, membrane

and tantrum, slow rubbing
like a scene of forms to cut

the scene they set because

I'm in the mood for love.

lindon barrett

elizabeth cotten

she put a statue of a surprise on the window sill. it was the size of a
chess piece. it smelled like a chess pie, rose up from itself in a dream
as festival music, for leftovers and late planning, till new years day's

excision curled exhaust, cut out, cut back, outlet, second, unthreaded,

a dusty veer on the avenue bus for the new survival of carolina statues.
she stayed at van gelder's, whose central fact was space, for seven years.
the material of poetry is so vast, she said, and we make delightful
instructions. we make them up by digging and chip away until we fall

in love with buried, made up things and understand that as a ghostly

matter. we fall in love with making plain confection, the taffy seriality

and braid to dig and dig and dig, then kept alive in phrasing for the
submarine, the beautiful way we go downstairs impossibly, and dig and
dig a hole in the open basement, happy with the feedback uncontrolled.
she had the snappy cereality of a little diving bird, and dig a hole for
gapped obstruction, sounding new black rice as a kind of candy, a public
fragment of a private strain, some scratched dirt on the off edge and dig.

her chorographic history of tuning upside down is uncanny and surreal,
the culinary marvelous wrapped up tight in brightleaf lace to breathe

for andrew cyrille, for kiril lakota, for evangeline's burnt cyrillic chord,
for uncalled for, unheard of in what they call for, out of breath in the
workmen's circle, the little books get cut and sewn that way to move
from warehouse to warehouse in reserve. little critical books with lines

to savor, microdances in held bodies in the warehouse, that turn out to

revive the warehouse, enthusiasm in the warehouse city, the little sewn

books of the low country, thrown in the air as little books of movement
of stone passage as liquid, arrangements on fire with the informal form
of the workmen's broken circle, flown out of looking ahead, walking for
the incidents, passage involved in our steps, in dressage, fallen like our
mothers, the fallen dance of mama and her commonness on fire, didn't
she send me any word, ain't she ready for the world? you see the ones

who know what it is to be prayed for. when they fasten up their little

transportation, the thing is how they all stay here. The complex word

of never to return makes them optimistic and pastoral. they give what
they do not possess—O, miracle of my life. we plan the commune as
epic instruments; we held in reverse for study and movement in safety;

we gathered all our little alls in four blocks of black notes. they were
hiding behind the counter at the corner store. in exorbitant small
bundles, the whole idea of the burst is a brand new start. for the ones
who can't start over, once again left with leaving as a kind of little all,

who raise a school up as the corner store, fill the shelf up with groove

habitation, the shrift and tide of black study in a cube or mass, in a

course of blown flare, a fanfare, Jacques Corsair, having flown, to begin

our studies of the little all, all held in counter, the under in Middleton's
black book, her new black mass and thrift habilitation, saving, sewing

music in the air, sown air in clothes and jewels for sacramental running,
for the soulfeast, for shift and stonefruit, her unknown constitution in a
highway that a ship stole, racked up in occult practice, to prayers in the
name of tabla and tamla, all and all's uncounted pulse to trade, gone in a

mellow dance, everybody long and sugar on the floor, soft coils in tore
up social density, turning in a violent chapel, a drive sound under a pier
for stepping out on quiet foil, edenton sung through hamlet in resolve,

the new general strike is jumpin! this is the flavor of our region, she said.
the regulators are breaking loose together and they still want us still, but
every amazing crush in us is that we got something prodigal, left out fold

and flight. running lines on the intercom, otolithic spirit photograph
still broken for the balance of our line to make it go right. we fold the
line in our own head and surge and stumble in the shadow. in slug's our

folded head bows down. we mime and trade in the everyday line, for the accident to hold down unreal chances, to stop running and staying away inside, once and for all, 'cause it's all right to have a good time. we were

thinking on the open lines and found a word we hid to start this new system of lines for you. will you and yours come see how much is hid in us? then you have to follow me away from you, come to yourself for

following the thing that's deep in you that comes up as a gesture for the

reindeer on your turquoise fleece, the little deictic pleasures of the

babies, the small textures of your cooking and the way you make me

copies of the new thing you keep listening to sometimes, how good of you to underrepresent. this is the music of my own head and you can hear it in the way I sound when I come away from that for you, twisted away in being folded up when I move away from that to turn my lines out for the other line inside. but let me stop beginning to let you come to this openness I hope for. hopefully it's forming itself from behind against just about every other folding you could think of just for you.

I want you to have this running away from you so you'll remember me

sometimes and love the way you let me get to you so I'm gon' really try

to make it good. will you be surprised again at who you are? I hope so 'cause it always makes me feel brand new to see you back to your old self, curling around in that extra way. maybe this will be open again as a great tightness that we drape around the world. yes, I do believe in the world, the edge, the stage is a complement and we are held together, saved, my love. that's all I've been wanting to show you along these lines.

nahum chandler

ann cvetkovich

music is numbers and feeling
when somebody goes something
like first. the scarce-saved something

sweet is nothing but the music.

there's a metaphysics of budget
that aspires to strings in the regular
broken mode so we hear for music

everywhere. we shook off the same time
with nothing but the serial appearance.
these solos are a birthday

to situate the bottom on a plane
through broken hills, the tone set

rhythmically, still frenzy, where soul is,
by the pool by the side of the road

kathleen stewart

frank ramsay

What can't be said, can't be said, and it can't be whistled either. It can't
be whispered. The burden can be muted. No wave and the barren
sequence rise on our account, triple soft but lashed, like in the first
instance, which can be sung. The right to love refusal is black music. The
song about desire always wants to disappear. In the second instance, she
released in public chastity, flirting at the club and wound. Damaged from
repeating, can you stay? Be my ontograph and discompose. If only you do
not try to utter what is unutterable then *nothing* gets lost. But the
unutterable will be — unutterably — *enjoyed* in what has been enjoyed.

nancy wilson

arthur jafa and greg tate

de anima: 2.16.8

all for our secret ends, the internal dispersion blew up local space. ohio
turned out to be a range of slide. soul is stare for decisive slide and

lounge, in advanced sub-cincinnati air, for all the unmade movies of all

our secret nomad ends, our devious monad ways. love the small bent

forms in movement's saturday night law library. there go off betty davis
with her paralegal shout. the magic precedent over somebody's house,
down up under where the magnolia volunteered to cut the overgrown
situation, parables on the verge as the burden of the gestic play we in,
having identified the shit, the shit you can't say shit about, that's all

I can say about that, had stayed in the bracket, flying. the blue beautiful
critic never really want to explicate himself from the underdeveloped
situation. the terror of enjoyment is *too* goddamn good. faded circular

pose, dyslexic swerve, the loop of out withdrawal inside this inextricable

song, the breakdown of all self-fashioning in hard singing, found in what

you found confected, d. j. caramel's open signature. it's most too tough
to imagine the cold, new history of somebody saying this is who I am.

joe torra

i. 'watching and listening'

make you dance in your head, off and

composed,   between black and white

tecture, fall and lifted flower tinted, overlaid grid drip or colored

vii. open association vacate   grid, my flag "Fred +
Laura,
viii. frame   to our
continued friendship w/Love
ix. meet
         Joe"
3. say yes. in. naw
4. (—)—>

7. "unfold drift

wood fishnet"

8. Light rips notes, shies.

10. the fall where marriage leaves

cascade possible and deviant

reframe. be ready for a breeze   'constant

disquisition'

11. sample,
sample
what sample
won't
13. barriers
         Chomsky.   "result
14. 'let me follow you again   evolve"
their bridges are barriers
now you say my playing is unwHAT?'

15.   attitude of the bridge
17. here

19. what's missing is the object of theory.

22. "under buoyancy"   everything the
absence of the punctuation mark can do is here. "over a wilderness": the
phrase or
23. |⁻⁻|⁻⁻|⁻⁻⁻⁻| word that marks a bridge
(barrier: there is punctuation here: black cross) but flows neither to
or lattice work   nor fro
beginning a refusal to sustain crochet
24. "the self unbridled encroach"
25. Johnny Hodges   open end not

dropped bomb

26. but then I glanced
at the tv screen a

daguerreotype of California
Indians long dead all

dead   her look pierces flashing

and she lays down   slither. strip   black

tape you get all that in New York

27. what happens is

that the serial

don't thicken but

blooms and intricates: Vienna. New Orleans. New York.
you get all that silence

of my head wild with
you all up in there

the line bursts in the

square's modesty   Milan, reading these poems,

talking with Ariel, on the bridge that is not a bridge

28. go back and check for water   "fracture an other"
can you understand a

painter's breath and your

own.
         flo Joe flow floy floy   flashbulbs
29. that's pretty music, boy.
31. that's perfect, huh?

piet mondrian

Charlie's tap was angled with fred
popky   of the elegant buzz, asking
burred and clipped

under the bottom and wrapt
ceiling, tin

rung, then the street fell, the repeating
barre, the bridge's shaft culture, like a pardoner's textural
bone, archaeology of black market
fountain saved for dancers

just tippin in *just tippin in*
with graphophone brush and hidden
air, as thornton dial,
a little empty space
with strangers for colored borders
in trained actors with

tape folded over
a common farm and move your form:

1. they are the   music in a little empty space 2. their
many heads now black in tavern sun since street life is a studio
and secret rent party and sub/urban scape committee

so come be in our play

3. the elegy and victory of

piet johnson and robert piet williams   is also stacked
with movement's austere jug   bottom land
in a dewdrop cave or a cave painted pool hall, in a

dissident cell and checkerboard lounge and
slide,
arrayed
in primary
buzz, for the common band of
wilke's scar, freda hopkins, bass.   53

nathaniel mackey

come from some of everywhere, somewhere so deep that some of
everywhere come with you. to become, for our occult belongings,

worldly in that other way, garnet burned in sand and long green shade

belonging in our garden. our feeling for the game is secret. harriott

is our conductor and our unfinished readiness for the world, occult and

separate mixture. that long revealed weave is come undone as our

unfinished readiness, the messed up plan of someone else's dance,
the celibate screen been a open window. you move the whole question
from room to room, echo chamber, our always ready unofficial word.

marie jenkins

wrong-angled faded striding lion
shattered whispered bone
on bone. stroll the way she won't

say she can't walk. slurred
but wiship, with brushes,
with her garden small,
and here I am.
she flew away to walk against
herself till the other morning.

         a competition for designing
the municipal hand rail
system of kingsland, arkansas
                    is announced
so she can stop again uptown
or where it used to be. Mimi was
a rhythm section.

what if she flung over Chitown like
gandelsonas pouring light over
Robt's house and Michaelsouse and Charlie's.
                    her fingers spann like folding
towers in Little Brother's house

and Al's. Frank's house. Irma's, Tine's,
Hubert Horatio Andrews. I can't
I can't I
can't singing
still live! sung prayers
gone but going, pedals bent, slung
prayers, she said, in stride

q. b. bush

[LOUISIANA CLUB]

open up some bright rhythm'o'
that bed against the wall. blood
some punch some straight sherm
sharp corner. like bobby's woman flew

from the dark left swinging,
we purred up in there, slung
and rolled the everynight form,
and that music messed me up,

that criminal repeating head.
like two piece of buffalo laid across

a piece of white bread or a boat

come across the window or

a train come over a scream

through new jerusalem

a layer beneath the service,
the gap between saturday and

sunday was a strip of tape on

paint, a motherfucking switchblade,
the dispossession of this other
motherfucker everyday by

albert carroll out the back of that white

station wagon, lounging in the door of
the pink apartment, walking to jail
across a empty lot, slipping out by
daybreak.

[COVE]

her juicy lips cut the enclose blowing stardust
digging in chains. the broke choir and
rolled light in the sound like bicho.

like a folded bird on the floor in the house,

like when the doctor said, "pearl, you ready to book?"

and was a tree we danced around that stayed
and glide, the spin was all about flying when you get cut

by mama's horn, then lay it down soft in the commons,

then play and listen like everybody else.

when she comes the fields start dancing rows
through walls, planters of leeks and stepped

up entertainers, leveled all the way out through

walls, wander knifelike like a blue method
from the lakes past the yellow birds cross 67 to

granddaddy on the other side of rainbow and

lake mead to the common room of 1948 north
d. the puritans with flavor say form a pit.

sleater-kinney

two lines twining all the time, look:
               the air, soft water (edge, animation

took the air out the window. I want

some travelers to come on in my kingsland.

got brokedown loops everywhere, broad novel
bright strings. got the holy ghost that

jesus is giving away for the undetectable sweet edge

                              this open house

with redbugs, red greyhounds, black

walnuts, where sharp bradleys and

whipporwills, great northerns and crowders
volunteer through the floor, the soil by
the milkglass, where plantation roped to
strings, to the mill blew up by every line
(fuse, tongue), is what I'm 'on get to

with mimi and laura in the fall, to water
flowers and polish and at four,

rise, in each way, hey mama, fugue and

edge, animation), to rip it up. blue silk
split the round fiber with a razor. buff a jagged
loop and fingertap. here go mimi the soft leather

keyboard here go mrs. parham with worry

here go mrs. owens' gone on solo.

eric dolphy

the ironworks on alameda. thala me

diron iron urn broke down. ironman

burned the factory, alamede brurned

like powder, like brush, what chord?

brokedown dalamede aburned hard

chunks of iron ash for pavement. alama
dea twirl cold down to la steel. two screams
announced the fire on the other side
of downtown this long-ass road. I know
one time I made a dancer's hand fly off,
foundry like powder, alamaquilladora orange
oran nogales. alamedid breakdown

is a fable, hard transfer, aleave in

nether, hard angle, low land, again,
said booker little, what corridor?

general baker

iggy pop and trisha brown. reset. reset and take a factory.
take the terminal of your factory if you think it's all that.
that from the sped-up line and train and dancers take and let
some montage of the alameda corridor blow up in toys cold
storage cans window glass cars roll like a film of capital

we finally got the news. we got the secret got object
shines take swing out that far and break the line you hold
hold like you hold the whole world in your hand all

that curved up music right when you both play and hold
the whole film and everybody hold that car you drive

we make the line dance and we design the set. we line
the dance up outside and irruption of plane plain song
blew the unit up to every level of association blew up cans
and toys and plate glass and paint the house and after all
brush and stroke cold storage signature vanish edge hell yeah

johnny cash

first diesel came through cuba
long possible hard stream to memphis

gravel on the edge of that black water

white flowers till that river black motel.

like making groceries at drake's on saturday

but no new lectronics of the sun. gotta get home to

that light by blind, slip through cotton plant
at night between the track and the river,

short sleeves but mo'nin' like a man with

a movie camera, but he took that hat off mystery,

dead slate brought back with friction. the sound
of the horn make the flat ones skim

till the edge and sharpen then red

then green then dyad then severed

                [politically man
                        dwells down here
                  in cubie

            that same train from dave cash

to the central valley. wood water asphalt steel pine

tremor flint michigan. fresh desert (cleared wood), out
from the center wheel but deep

in that high social cotton, social
ground, I don't know when,

whistle smoke drive on.

this diesel came thu kingsland then dyess on severn

trumpeters thought about gabriel
maybe they heard it like sunshine

honey bee heard it like sunshine

baby b mine like sunshine

rosetta tharp

pam grier

caught up in between effort

and loss of touch in the fitting room

but just for a hot minute.

                          shoulder

fade delicate and every clap

ends with a brush stroke, a turned

e, silhouette know she fine, file
called yes I can.

if you try you can see her
nose veer, shit like that,
slew foot. I got to have

them shoes. you used to call me bobby

you used to whisper day to day

fight but I hear her saying

angel eyes, come on hold
the swing and cut o this b and
then went back to school.

bobby bland

either in shadow torso
if the red line machine
here go that hole in the street

mute all the yellow fabric
open the hollow shaft

here go that hole in the street

touch in my red-ass ears
whispering red black salt
here go that hole

in the air of every solid

all them first things
open head and mask

all of them plain tunes
every broke tone and flew
every squall all broke

weather every hole
here go that hole last

tape in the deck every

chain here go that chain
here come that street and slide
here go that hole in the street

la niña de los peines

off-edge a delicate weight. breath
and the load shifted. the arabesque
chord was acid. her throat was torqued
and small. her dance floor was a point

it's a little alone

booble knows that a wave is a touch
and swallow, come back as laughing
on a secret painting, on the secret span,
flashing, casta, castanet and brush

laura harris

gaps just sped by as I remembered, but now I live in my open days,
after the end between bird and track, irrupted always

and everywhere from laura beth harris, it's a little alone, holding up the
window, light

swishing in the frame like Finnegan's orange tail, his orange trail.

song for is fantasia, not faded, proposition stashed in paper in wax,
other tablets sugar and stone,
but you sang from the platform, piercing my proposal,

the utopian jew of voice.

but not covering. it's a little alone

through Newark, looking for a big red house and out towards New
Brunswick and out towards Princeton, but before and under all that

whistling, break and shudder for planned explosions, predatory

contracts, red attacks in the eyes, sticking through my fingers, to the

desert in Philadelphia. it's a little alone

for returning, I was reliving, just running underground to see the icons
glow, coming off the word and resolved to do this other thing,

sharp, dark, out fury like the shadow of a project sprawled in gray,
the static cube, where the sand blow by, where they brought them tanks

that time, it's a little alone

it's slow. smoke chips off painted brick and haze engraved on the body of the one who taste it.

Darryl, say Durl, say Lonnell of the popular garden, get down
offa of that train.

brang take glance suitcase hand *aw why don't you glance down/at your*

wedding band it's slow. the brownsville architecture opens up a long
construction of the window which is

image, recirculated air, whisper and tongues, caress the fucked-up city,
the lovebird call, the utopian jew of voice.

Hemphill died today

in my ear, in bronzeville, underneath an arc on the ground, bluiett said

"see," how my hand twists, "this

sounds beautiful to me," broke the chamber, the horn's edge, like
chipware of the new instrument, its
anatexture,

hopelessly figuring the way back under the hollow stanchion of a scarry
bridge. it's a little alone

it's a little alone. who's playing tonight

will twist her reddened hand into a letter. my orchestra, will you slide?
the withered bridge blew movement as a heavy load

as Hemphill's fluttered, raptured body,
and Olu Olu Wadud, d, wadud, du du Olu, du, de novo, muted, bell,
Dara, leap, as
service, whose

arc was kickin on a thing called "laura and the city, laura in the city's
what I woulda called it, a fantasia." it's a little alone

now here I am, monks surround me, we are pillows for each other, to
ride this train, it's a little alone

revue, resistance flew to this complaint and here I am
with you and ours

in the long broken line of the breathing circle,

in the general rain, it's a little alone
but you brushed on me and sang (the utopian view of joyce, who did my
mama's nails, who comes through

broken records, who made the record turn, who broke the old

construction, who recovered), I remembered, in the opening

betty carter

hard daydream, ribbons chatter, it's dejohnelle,
bright vein and shells. johnny shines and crying

panther in the middle of the highwayside.

like the burnt speech of this set but   (she was four swayed fingers

folded down; now step! but)   they would
brush up on each other

for signals and nearness but she hold it all up in
that arch her lips curl and ridge and it just
seem like her hand fold the fold of your neck, how

she lay out over there around on dropping things
it's a little alone it's a little alone it's a little alone

william corbett

[OWE YOU A LETTER]

late between poem and something

way over into april springtime rain
and song washing wave after dust of sun
in the season of the listening party

in the real high wisdom of his colors

dutchman and the flower's names

the cover of a spare full collection

"To Bill, Philip '77 unworded
marks of the outside he takes in:
I wanted to say I'm with you
been reading Hank Jones painting

looking at the edge of ensemble
to say that I been calling try
and sing with you on all occasions

[BUILDING, SONG AND FLOWER]

looking and window is

there hollow flower a
trumpet. its the wind

in a yellow garden.
look at fairfield porter, I'm

a look at them play that

think I heard valentine.
look don't, but the corner

is sharp. the granite. one
sees this that in porter

blue is garden the brush
like a cluster loves the tone

make sound like thickness.
got to think about that
'cause you do it Bill

real pretty
love

Fred

june jordan

pearl   tear

pear   tear

heat lore flown flow flare

or

fleet fore gone here there

pier mere pearl flew tear

reet pear through tear bore

sweet true lore flow quair

murray jackson

the pure attachment of

I heard a negro play the

circle. working high uphorn
back under mixing jones

ruption lesion lision

sit in the wind the

sittin winds, the window

home and uptown
henderson, windsor

organize this breeze

cool this last dish

just leave a swallow
and save some pie

then keep it short

paint their feast day

conjugate that
quickness off to
new happiness

to new happinesses.

how ya' doin', man?

as little as possible.

curtis mayfield

[BEEN WITH YOU ALL THE TIME]

on the greyhound
under the slant
I saw dark matter

on the radio, telescope.

chicago is some hard rows and
dirty bone: she give
essays on objects and events: a
queen

        like josephine baker checking the fly patchwork of her land,

riots jacking the edge of doors, her tongue in his mouth animating his

axe, algeria's tongue in france's mouth, my heart has a

mouth in it, face of the blue heart, history of the custom,

history of the unbuilt project, what it documents
of the blow it up, history of the push, history of the
transfer of substance, break the stage in the
singing glance, canting, incline, span, jargon, long row

[PEOPLE MUST PROVE TO THE PEOPLE]

a modular blue public at the common sing is under the café,
in daniel carter's interlocking lofts of buried sets,

small circles, tendrils, hard rows, secret passage, sphere,

brokedown stereo, leaked privacy,

multivocal general leakage. the set nonviolently was a street corner.

never let anybody say that we can't break true,

dirty bone, green glass, new gather,
every corner just a shock like it's posed to be.
lick lick quick that blue version, blend in a festival of openers,

can hear everything but your fingers are free
to cut the adoration of the jack-leg, doubleness
of the inside, name the black ordinary after all this time by side long
row.

[HISTORY OF THE CURTOM]

the bridge is a tilted arc on tilted song.
like authenticity is an asymptotic relation.
like dance is a natural object.
like blackness move the human to impossible end.

like madness of the work is blue present in this mad unformed.

like knowledge of the instrument along a more than singular register.

when was the assertion of blackness anything other than interrogation,

the question event, hard rows, where you going girl, in the sweetness of,

the event that never happened, restored but never publicly

presented? what's the difference between the morning and the evening
star? fallen, feel the breakdown of the body that was already there,
the distance from itself, its own folded decay, and open up some

brightness bluer than dark dark hat bluer than straw darker

than bluer than red and black back to the bridge keep on long row

carrie tirado bremen

Blues is deflected in Gayl Jones. Blues is defected, the broke musical

assemblage of the mobile asylum. This complex of light and sound
is refraction, as matter glancing, indirected, address bent to the bent

impossibility of address, my dear, language folded up on something

more than communication, when communication is impossible and

then it intimates, spookily acting out on you at a distance; this foliation

of narrative in and against an infertile, imposed fertility of narrative, its

straight line reproduction, ungathered point to point, no clearing, no

hollow, no project chapel, as if I could only be if I was you; this light

waved goodbye and curve sounded, chromatic brushes on the edge of

war and that libertine inmate jam, cool in plans the architect can't hear,
new rooms breaking out of gates, who is the architect's faithless servant.

Topological jones is like tropological jones but gone, badder than a hog

need slop, the comic race on the cosmic bus, just keep on trucking

blackness to the end of the in-between line, before the baroqueness of
the blues' black notes (is there a baroness of the blues? Yes. Gayl Jones).

margaret walker

the problem is for my people than blue then
orange and shoreline of the common reservoir.

there's a wasteland for another spring
they wait on. water misrecognized
for sky. edgeshifting seeing what
you want to see pointing curving

making common of another habit.
an arc falls in and out of light like this

this late. the yellow bill on my blue

cap. the purple handle of a blue

bag. to make up for the content edge

shifting into flavor the same way they
slipped off at night sometimes escaping
counting to the next hard row they keep on

making commons. it don't make sense not to
keep on pushing, to the edge of things, for silk

audre lorde

audre lorde

traced back from whirr
and interrupted again
brushes to a scar

that's already risen

from what won't be there
when you keep on looking
till day after tomorrow
and come up missing

in mozelle's full black

outskirts and how she fold

up broken affect in
play mama's long escape,

this hard open look out
and over, all up under all

this, but out from, the
other thing, from her. here.

kara keeling

chrisshonna grant

cruise erzulie, blue across the water,
up and down the street with pretty flowers.

azule scrape as usual. the seraphim
another set from blue across and julian

curl away from separate to pause

it's a little alone

and watch her cross and re-cross central avenue

blue train. the social culture crash

from cross morgan and fuller but sure

as the broken line of blue alternates. when they ran
back home she used it for another ring

that's hid up underneath a broken shift
made out of pretty flowers. a bunch of new

people trying to grow old vegetables
till they can run back home. trying to grow
field peas in cement, wrapt in a blue shawl.

victor feldman

toni morrison

                         till it feel some better

           prose such and such
                 "write off to the side"   and not too much

renee gladman

              it's a little alone

njeeri wa ngugi

in the world to scream against

the invading encloser, always crossing
past return, an advent. we were here

before the sad absences. we are philosophical

contraband. our braid flew off the

circle from inside like a pathogenic

bass line. the point of the counterband
was the other ones. like the Prophetess

Amanda Irving praying for the

lost ones, in protest, committing
thy body to the bass line, in

turning reading everything,

it gives me pleasure to ask that you
pray for me before we raise the broken city

to make another world

john work

genre is window service
in concert with driving

the long withdrawn thing

named come disturb us.

the second secret purpose
of the field recording
is theory. what they bring

is rigorous and marvelous

so get some. whirl & cuss

till the symposium sing

the intentional curving
of the quartet omnibus

volume with fluxus; vor
lesen till understanding
fade like a broken ring

of fire. is it perverse

how strong my love is?

that it's as strong
as that's how strong

my love is? preserve us.

barbara lee

Even since Plato, some poets remain surprised that they don't run shit, that they ain't even citizens. But black poetry suffers its politics of non-exclusion. Abide with this distress for the deformative and reformative stress, the non-normative benefits, the improper property of the ones who have been owned, who are without interests, who are feared, who disappear in plain, excaped, unfree.

Counterinsurgency only ever offs the possibility incompletely. A state of race war has existed with its immense poetry of tread water, worked ground, houses sawed in half. That's where the socially off hold on, try to enjoy themselves.

There is a history of the embrace of degraded pleasure. Poetry responds, cantedly, to the slander of motivation. Poetically man dwells, amped, right next to the buried market, at the club underneath the quay, changing the repeat, thrown like a new thing, planning to refuse until the next jam, at a time to be determined and fled.

Poetry investigates new ways for people to get together and do stuff in the open, in secret. Poetry enacts and tells the open secret. Getting together and doing stuff is a technical term that means X. Something going on at the sight and sound center of sweet political form.

[STATEMENT IN OPPOSITION]

speaker, members,
heavy, but risen
through muted,
I had to rely on
the inside songs.
welcome to the same
new world. I, the
runaway, say don't go
off. somebody blew
us up. welcome
to the state of
mourning. come
look at the difficult
broken flesh. stay
a little while. don't
let him do what
he just did. suffer
with me tonight
in my native hue.
I want to be the
opposite.

[THE UNACKNOWLEDGED LEGISLATOR]

According to Shelley, poets are the unacknowledged legislators of the world. Let's say the world is a zone from and within which life is constantly escaping. Poets sing the form of that endless running, that ongoing running on, always busting out of the sentence or cutting being-sentenced; but those broken songs, even in their incessant breaking away, cannot but bear the heavy burden of being-held. At stake, here, is a complex of weighted departure, of flight in seizure, of an emergent statelessness submerged beneath the state of emergency. There's always a trace on the ones who want to go. Nevertheless, unacknowledged legislators sing diversion out of turn. They instigate small passages. Their envois strive to more than correspond.

Somewhere between being one of the elect and having been elected, the unacknowledged legislator operates on the edge of things, resisting that desire for inclusion that eviscerates politics-as-the-politics of escape. When brutal attacks on the simultaneously real and symbolic centers of brutal power constitute a reactive, reactionary chance to open the books of legitimate anti-politics, so that associates can become made men, the unacknowledged legislator chooses to remain unmade and unacknowledged. The maker remains unmade even when she is subjected, momentarily, to the glaring hyper-visibility intermittently trained on the ones whose differences periodically re-initialize ante-politics. Veering off from state-sanctioned rhetorical reserves and out of national pseudo-humanist discursive frames, her sound reveals that she is thinking and, therefore, marginal; and that she keeps thinking about what it means to be on the outskirts or part of the outwork of the Republic. But she is, at the same time, constrained to offer her musicked speech in the already given idiom of anti-politics. Her veering off from and out of occurs inside, in the name of that other, outer interiority. So she turns what is turned against into a vestibule, an ante-room. She takes this turn in a cramped, cracked stanza, homelessly acting like she at home by taking flight, held still in forced movement. That weight compels the unacknowledged legislator to love (the way to get to) what hasn't happened yet, to care for the way what hasn't happened yet is in the midst and on the edge of its negation, to turn in and on negation's language until it comes out, if not comes out right, as ante-nation language.

This language that is before the nation is, finally, more than international. In this sense, unacknowledged legislators aspire to be real ambassadors. The ante-national language of diplomacy is a bent poetics in which the one who inhabits a history of displacement speaks the ethics that attend that history by way of interstitial jargon, tones and fragments that get under the skin of the standard, words and phrases that slip or seep into the underground of the *patria*, that re-emerge as a set of broken claims to patriotism or a set of claims breaking patriotism, depending on how you hear. This off- or sub- or super-standard poetics links political speech to songs for distingué lovers or other such distressed, seemingly simple gifts. What is left to the listeners, the strangers, the ones who will have gone on to practice or to rehearse this music, this poetry, this poetics, is a general responsibility of advance, where what it is to move on is all about having gone back into and under the ark of displaced social life, that outer space structured by inner sound, which is where the poetics of political form lives, where that poetics takes up and is taken up by its life, which is a form of life, cloaked, clothed, veiled, given in a sumptuary law of motion. The unacknowledged legislator is ante-American, secreted in the raiment that loved flesh secretes. This aura of the dispossessed is owned shade, claimed shadow, the wrapt shawl of the poor.

The unacknowledged legislator is Barbara Lee.

mike davis and glynda white

She always already ready to be fresh off somebody's ass. Late at night
when she watch them slur our broken homelessness and slip a tape in to

tape it she also be always writing on the endless block of notepad what

she'll say to whichever one mess with her tomorrow. She can't really

walk no more but she always too ready to jump on somebody. She stay

ready to fight the jack-leg president and his brutal, optic jones when she
recline to renew her other aspiration for that gone off singing all this

ongoing mutual aid and how we fill it up with light in the underground.

Knowing everybody, she bout to decide to go into detection. A music-
filled wall at work is her bulletin board. Into the richness of the gone

off, there's an opposite gallery of injured workers that she sees about.

Her enforcement officer is Mike and he'll fuck you up twice if it come
to that. Her attorney is Ms. White, whose brilliance is the courthouse
parking lot. Under special circumstances she ride over to 1948 N. "D"

to consult the first lady of soul and the funky president. She paralyze

whoever steal the swamp cooled air and put 'em on a brand new sign.

charlie parker

the circle laura of agoura
the circle lore my circuit girl
wanna move in your beauty.
this is sad. my transport's no one

else's name like gilmore can't hold

immense blue immense sweet

heavy but that don't work but
the shit is beautiful as if its sign
was you

        that cut me but I swerved my line

the line of cars separates like glass
the glass separate and fix the smile
the 101 drips down. a word

with our sound melody and class

is now the set of past the set—a bird.

pure downness of a seal and go

shadow of a pure feel which is

your finger in my hand your hand
softening my reel and cut your
real and blow and you relieve

being above every possible mark
and unmark beautiful in the clear

wind beautiful then pierce
beautiful and extreme

camarillo

birdia mott

dairy lingers through information

then panther creek. from pine

tree to round green. the green is

round 'causa work and wish then

slope down to that trinkle tinkle
accidental bridge. at the end of a
chute of softwood round green

curve down to the edge of some

soft, hidden water. the patches indicate

savor, the cows stay put, their backs
are the bottom of a curved frame. st. james

flattens out to miss b.c.'s little

rise and on to rison and pine bluff.
this is the beginning and end of my
trumpeter's round trip, blue
butterfly, green round as her
smile and sound. hey mama,

check out this new

julian djibril

imperfect beat, no tonic, not at home,
the bravado of your vibe and that inside
smile got me running up and down the street
saying look, look, look inside my bag!

see how muted he is on the outskirts
of the new modal auxiliary city, my gerbil,

bent chroma of the girl who sold the sun,
little cheeks puffed out like a little cannonball?

already defending yourself from rough kisses,

come carrying your own sign in the first place,

new ensembles calling for you every night

'cause word is out about the way you straighten up.
last night your big mama told me all about you—
"what waits for after the mind can't imagine"

lorenzo bird

seven twenty two seven o nine with hands with something to say is
mysterious broken with happiness lorenzo conducting.
can't tell you how much

(but my voice mimes me.

there is escape in there
like an island grain

that my voice sounds for
and the sound is me
but it's not me)
it's a little alone

the break the object
the bridge the panther walks

the bridge at panther creek

the cuban son of arkansas

the madrigal of cubie booms

the eight track of q. b.
the train of things

the field and ash across
the other yellow room the sonnet drum
(but my voice mimes)

the sound came from the other one the broken thing
the separate and touch slant and churn

the feather bed remember

the hands far away inside laura (my city) and me.
this is your picture book and

transport pastoral little hawk

little ren little noam little harms little

gandy little isaac hayes little friend little b

my little alone little enzo the baker come to help your father

so they can sing your line just by glancing

your hands move the history of movement

and taking and holding the song insists.
you say "I'm gone but you come with me"

and paint your other name
gift lightning message clearing near arrow cluster walker broken

morning element strain cutlass traveler manual opening curve

fred hopkins

booms, b, but the circle strays
to the docks. stretch and slice but
tied a string around. strain against
walking. she say them kids

delicious. could mama had'a tried

less hard if she'd'a strayed. that stay

against walking had to fall. the heavy

weight of that black thang shattered:

that buzz underneath muhal by mcbee, that wide-

ass tie from mr. b's, that secret password

in the name of mr. b, that big fat brown
ray brown gone stray and stayed fell down and strain
and round and smile, that green sound, them

beautiful kids, their round needles,
murray jackson, fred hopkins, b jenkins

b jenkins

just so you know, no one could have told me you didn't want to go
outside. this exercises phonograph to take the receiver and call you
for something we hear together, some of the same stories, some of the
same things. to stretch repeat so thin it fades to various is the aim of
the phone call. the phonograph is also a photograph of movement and
what it bears. you found dances waiting for dancers. your silhouette is
patient form. I know you can cant. I know you can make it if you try.

I'm getting along alright. I say a little prayer. mama's baby sadie mae
ms. davis' blue and red. at the duck inn mighty lions roar. you and
bobby bradford run away together. this earth tone air is b.c. marks's
pine bluff arkansas, asleep in new pajamas at the desert inn, to walk
joe williams pieceway home to waycross, you and me against the world,
every time we say goodbye. I'll be seeing you in all the unfamiliar places
where they till our long advance. this is the cluster song of our romance.

"Words Don't Go There"

AN INTERVIEW WITH FRED MOTEN
Charles Henry Rowell

This interview was conducted by telephone on June 23, 2004, between College Station, Texas, and Los Angeles, California, where Fred Moten resided with his family.

ROWELL: You are one of those rare academics; you are a poet as well as a literary and cultural critic. In each of the sites you occupy, you attempt to engage audiences through written and spoken words. But each of these sites, we often contend, requires particular ways of speaking that we assume are different—and, in some instances, are directly opposed to each other. We definitely argue that these two forms of communicating—criticism and poetry—are produced by different sensibilities, and what results are two distinct forms of communication—one critical and the other creative. This has led, of course, to contemporary critics ignoring contemporary literature, especially poetry, and contemporary writers not reading contemporary critical texts. Where do you stand in this divide? Or should I ask the question this way: How do you negotiate the two sites you occupy—that of "high" theorist and that of "experimental" poet?

MOTEN: I don't think I'm that rare, partly because the folks who have been the most influential for me operate precisely within that dual mode and partly because those who have influenced me have influenced many others as well. Amiri Baraka and Nathaniel Mackey have been and remain extremely important to me. They   97 are both deeply embedded in the commitments and protocols of a strain of American poetic experimentalism that goes back to Whitman and Dickinson and that includes seminal figures like Ezra Pound, William Carlos Williams, Charles Olson, and Robert Duncan. Like all of these writers, Baraka and Mackey find it necessary to make contributions to poetics to ground and justify the kind of deconstructive and reconstructive pressure they put on poetic norms. Their poetry and their writing about poetry always reveals how hard and how seriously they think about the nature of poetry in its relation to the world and to history. That kind of thinking must be an intensely theoretical endeavor; it brushes up against and infuses and is infused with the kind of thinking that people usually consider philosophical. So that there are some "high theoretical" tones that mark both the poetry and the poetics of, say, Olson or Duncan and those tones or their variants are evident all the time and everywhere in Baraka and Mackey. Moreover, Baraka's engagement with German philosophers such as Martin Heidegger, Ludwig Wittgenstein, and Karl Marx, and Mackey's encounter with contemporary French theorists like Julia Kristeva and Jacques Derrida are also very evident in their work, giving it a whole other kind of theoretical or critical intensity. And this is all in the service of a deep immersion in the massive theoretical demands and resources of Afro-diasporic art and life. So that the two writers who have the most immediate and lasting influence on me move in the necessity of a breakdown of the oppositions between poet and critic, experimentalist and theorist, from within the complexity of the Afro-diasporic cultural field. And their critical extension of their own multiple lines of origin just lays down tracks for the future investigations of a whole lot of others (as Hortense Spillers, another great poet-critic, might say). So many names come to mind; it's hard to think of all this in terms of rarity, and it's hard to think of the divide between high theory and experimental poetry as an especially unusual one to negotiate.

ROWELL: When one looks at your poems, one discovers a new texture of English, or one finds a struggle toward language, or one is revealed the inadequacy of English to render all you want to say. (It's even difficult for me to fashion the exact phrase or sentence to describe, with certainty, the linguistic field of your poetry. [Laughter.]) "Words don't go there," as Charles Lloyd is reported to have said when he was asked to comment on one of his musical compositions. Actually one might be inclined to say the same about some sections of *In the Break: The Aesthetics of the Black Radical Tradition*, especially the section on Cecil Taylor. Some of the writing there reminds me of your poems. I would not be surprised if you have written a poem on the subject of that section of *In the Break*.

MOTEN: It's true that a lot of the objects of inquiry in my critical work are objects of inquiry in my poetry as well. My wife, Laura Harris, has been working on the relation between experimental and documentary aesthetic forms, on what it means for artists and critics to consider both as modes of inquiry, and this has had a big influence. She has really transformed the way I think about and write poetry. Writing a poem has become for me, at least in part, an attempt to find out some things and to try to work through some things intellectually, emotionally, and musically. I'm trying to find out some things, get at some things, and consider some things, while at the same time trying to make some things. That process is a struggle toward language that tries to struggle toward things; it is movement in preparation. In *In the Break* I refer to Eric Dolphy talking about preparing himself to play with Cecil Taylor: I'm trying to write in preparation, as well; maybe not to play with Cecil but to abide with his work better or more fully, to listen more carefully and creatively and critically. For me, this sense of writing as preparation or even anticipation constitutes something on the order of a mode of inquiry. And this gets us back to some issues that are embedded in your first question, issues concerning the differences and the relations between modes of inquiry (the poetic and the critical, the experimental and the theoretical). Many of the folks I write about in *In the Break*—Billie Holiday, Adrian Piper, James Baldwin, Dolphy, Taylor, and, probably above all, my late mother, B. Jenkins—I have written poems about as well. There are thematic and stylistic gaps between these modes of writing/inquiry but the connections probably far outweigh them. I think these connections are getting stronger, more pronounced in my work, but, at the same time, I'm still deeply committed to maintaining the distinction between the two modes and to the notion that they are both indispensable in this preparation for, or struggle toward, things. So I've been thinking a lot about that distinction, how to inhabit it and trouble it at the same time and in the interest of things. The difference between a poem "about"

Lady Day and a chapter on her in a more properly critical or theoretical text might emerge in the poem's challenge to syntactic or semantic norms, in its going after a sound that might not get you where the word or the sentence gets you, but might get you past the word's or the sentence's limits or, even better, might take the word or the sentence past its own limits. It's not so much that a critical text might allow me to say this while a poem might allow me to do this; it is, rather, that they can both be beautiful ways both to say and do this. What Lady does to the words (and the sentence)—"Don't explain"—explains everything. Anyway, I think that the oppositions between theory and experiment, poetry and criticism, are constraints that enable us when we resist them and when we resist the urge simply to obliterate them. In the end, I want my criticism to sound like something, to be musical and actually to figure in some iconic way the art and life that it's talking about. At the same time, I also want my poetry to engage in inquiry and to intervene, especially, in a set of philosophical and aesthetic questions that are, I think, of profound political importance. This is, for me, a specifically Afro-diasporic protocol.

ROWELL: I am fascinated by your description of poetry as "a mode of inquiry." Will you say more about that in relation to two of your poems, "Other Dimensions in Music, Ghostcatching"* and "Johnny Cash/Rosetta Tharp"?

MOTEN: "Other Dimensions in Music, Ghostcatching" is a poem I wrote in New York when I was teaching in the Department of Performance Studies at New York University. That is to say, I was in a kind of intellectual transition from more and less traditional literary critical methods to the very different kinds of attention that the study of performances and the theorization of performance demand. One of the big questions in which I found myself immersed at that time was this: "Where do performances go?" If you think about it as a kind of independent partner to the question concerning the fate of words that Charles Lloyd (and, by way of Lloyd, Nathaniel Mackey) addresses a whole lot of interesting things open up, all of which depend upon your dealing with the imperative to go and see (and hear) performances. So in New York I attended lots of performances while always thinking—by way of the work of my colleagues in Performance Studies, José Muñoz, May Joseph,

* *Hughson's Tavern* (Providence: Leon Works, 2008), 83.

Barbara Browning, Diana Taylor, André Lepecki, Peggy Phelan, and Richard Schechner—about the fate of those performances after they were gone. I wanted to figure out a way to write (about) these performances, to record them, without killing them or capturing them. I also wanted to think about performances as modes of inquiry and as modes of writing to see how a kind of recording was already embedded in them. This seemed like precisely the kind of constellation of issues that demanded lingering in the break between poetry and criticism, experiment and theory, and that's the place "Other Dimensions" comes from and lives in. But all that's just a preface. The poem is a recording of two performances. The first part of the title is simply the name of a wonderful quartet—consisting of trumpeter Roy Campbell, saxophonist Daniel Carter, bassist William Parker, and drummer Rashid Bakr—that I saw and heard one night at a club called Tonic in the lower East Side. The second part of the title refers to an experiment in improvised choreography and new technologies of motion capture and animation performed by Bill T. Jones and digital artists Shelley Eshkar and Paul Kaiser. I was able to see their work and the story of the putting together of their work when it was installed at the Cooper Union. The material of the poem is those performances, my reaction to them, and my desire to record them (a desire mediated by debates in performance studies about the relation or no relation between liveness and recording). At a certain point, I guess, the necessarily fragmented notes I took during the performances and the cut-up memories I scrambled to transcribe after the performances were given over to a poem rather than an essay by way of a process or a decision that I'm still trying to get a handle on. At the same time, I'm aware of the trace of those performances in the critical work in which I'm now engaged and certainly the juxtaposition of the words—"motion" and "capture"—so resonant in Jones's dancing and in his reticence toward the very form of Ghostcatching, so central to the Afro-diasporic philosophical and aesthetic assertion, has become fundamental to that work. And the performance of Other Dimensions in Music always kept this issue of movement's relation to confinement—this time in its relation to the production of sound—alive. Daniel Carter's torso bending and twisting after notes so strenuously as to suggest an attempt to wrench himself away from his own firmly planted feet seemed to cross over into the Pentecostal quickening of Jones's hands and breath, however weighed down they were by the very instruments (of restraint: wires, relays, a special suit) that made his choreography, his movement-writing, possible. I wanted to get in on all this phonochoreography, to think about or amplify and illuminate the movements that were produced to make music and the movements that the music produced; I also wanted to ask some questions about the relationship between artist and audience as well as that between performances that are discrete in terms of time, space, and genre. "Johnny Cash/ Rosetta Tharp" is concerned with a lot of the same things though the personal connections are of a different order. Cash and my mother were both born in a small town in southeastern Arkansas called Kingsland. Early in his childhood Cash moved north to Dyess, Arkansas, a cotton-farming community near Memphis. His family was part of a New Deal experiment in which poor farmers were given a plot of land to work in a kind of cooperative arrangement with other farmers that was mediated and enabled by the federal government. In one of his autobiographies Cash speaks fondly of growing up under socialism. I was thinking of that particular experiment while listening not only to Cash but to Sister Rosetta Tharp, who was born in a place called Cotton Plant, Arkansas, which is not too far from Dyess. All kinds of associations came to mind, some of which I tried to make room for in the poem, however obliquely: my cousin Jacqueline who has taught school in Cotton Plant for thirty years; Jerry Eckwood, a great running back from nearby Brinkley, Arkansas who played for the University of Arkansas Razorbacks; the trains that run back and forth through Cash's music and through much of the music of the Mississippi/Arkansas Delta. I imagined a train moving from Kingsland to Dyess, the sound of the horn of the first diesel that came through Kingsland and how my mother told me that she thought it was Gabriel on Judgment Day; I thought about how the part of Kingsland that she—and later, for a couple of years, I— lived in was called Cuba (pronounced Cubie) by my great Uncle Eli because the neighborhood's fugitive nocturnal goings-on corresponded to what he'd heard about Havana. I wanted to imagine in a new way the commerce between musics that emerge from underground, experimental, stolen collectivities, and I wanted to approach it in a poem that was precisely trying to work through this kind of complicated being together. This poem, as well as "Other Dimensions," investigates and tries to sound and move with some old and new ensembles (of different musical traditions and social constructs, of public histories and secret personal reference).

ROWELL: Your comments anticipate my next question. Without the background information you have given us on those two poems, we, as readers, by the absence of helpful information, cannot acquire a full experience of a great number of your poems. And yet you cannot—and should not—give us a gloss of the personal or private elements of each of your poems. Is it appropriate for me to ask you to give us, however brief you'd like to make them, some helpful comments or notes on how we might read or experience your poems? And I apologize for such a sophomoric question/request.

MOTEN: It's not a sophomoric question; it's a very difficult question, too hard to answer directly. My first chapbook was called Arkansas, a title that the publisher, my friend and teacher William Corbett, realized was appropriate before I did. I sent a copy of it to my mother when it first came out, a couple of months before she passed away. She called me on the phone one day and said, basically, that she didn't know what was going on in these poems. She told me that every once in a while she saw a name or something that she recognized but that what she didn't recognize was the poetry as poetry or, at least, as the kind of poetry she'd had to read in school. She would say, "You know, I had to read poetry in school. And by the way I didn't like reading poetry in school when I had to read it, but I know from reading that poetry that yours is not like that. So what are you doing?" One of the things that I tried to say to her was that I grew up in her house, a house infused with music, including the music of the speech of the people in that house and in my neighborhood. I wanted my poetry to record and amplify that music. But I also wanted to change that music. Now I think that amplifying and transforming that music is done by way of something that already lies at that music's very heart. This root seems to me to be unavailable and secret, like a chain of receding events, any one of which might fool you into calling it an origin. It is, nevertheless, there and one prepares to get at it by going out. There is a reading of Mackey and Spillers and Baraka and Samuel R. Delany that I have been engaged in and that I hope is just and that reading was my guide. That kind of movement—Mackey would call it "centrifugal"—is inseparable, I think, from a certain desire for misrecognition, but I have to say that it was hard on me for my mom not to recognize herself or her music in my poetry. We talked about it for a long, long time. We communicated a lot that day about failing to communicate and I like to think that there was something in the poems, independent of shared references and even of the fact that I was her son, that made her think it was worth it to read them. There might be only a few folks for whom the poems seem worth it (not in spite of but because of their failure or refusal to communicate). But I would say to those folks that I hope that they can, or will try to, recognize some music that they know in my poems. But all this is just another mournful preface. Okay. Here's something I wrote really early this morning. "There is a kind of pressure that music and poverty (constraint) puts on the sentence; the remainder (flight) is poetry. Over the course of history the demands of truthful expression (as either or both correspondence and discovery) become more and more severe, but at the same time 'the plain sense of things' becomes more plain and the striated polyvocality of the vessel, the medium, the conductor, strives for directness." I think poetry is what happens or is conveyed on the outskirts of sense, on the outskirts of normative meaning. I'm trying precisely to work on that edge, and I assume that the content that is conveyed on that edge, on that fault line, is richer, deeper, and fuller than those things that are given in writing that passes for direct. That's definitely a kind of prejudice of mine—and I could be wrong. The art that always threatens the boundaries of sense has been the art that has been the most beautiful for me. What I love about Schoenberg or Olson is not the same thing as what I love about my cousin Reverend L. T. Marks's sermons, but it's nothing other than that either. I want my poems to carry that weight, and part of what I do to accomplish this is to maintain a wide range of reference. And while certain names or titles—or certain phrases or breaks in phrasing—might not resonate for every reader, what I'm hoping is that the music I'm trying to make with that name or by way of certain tones or images that are part of the composition and that I associate with this or that proper name will come through. So that the kind of embedded experimentalism in both the ceremonial and the everyday speech of my cousin corresponds in rich and interesting ways to a set of issues and a set of problems that I've been trying to work through by way of the critical theory that I've been reading. I want my poems to be a musical effect of encountering Marx and Marks and of the encounter between them in my work—of their impossible communication of the new possibilities of communication that might occur as a function of courting miscommunication in general and of this miscommunication in particular. So I'm depending on the kindness of strangers (and friends to whom I make unsolicited submissions!) toward stuff that I know is not for everybody even though I'm trying to make it for everybody. In the end, however, as Saidiya Hartman says, "the right to obscurity must be respected." This is a political imperative that infuses the unfinished project of emancipation as well as any number of other transitions or crossings in progress. It corresponds to the need for the fugitive, the immigrant and the new (and newly constrained) citizen to hold something in reserve, to keep a secret. The history of Afro-diasporic art, especially music, is, it seems to me, the history of the keeping of this secret even in the midst of its intensely public and highly commodified dissemination. These secrets are relayed and miscommunicated, misheard, and overheard, often all at once, in words and in the bending of words, in whispers and screams, in broken sentences, in the names of people you'll never know. I'm trying to write the poetry of riding the bus in the city. What keeps this from being bare romanticism (I hope) is the misunderstanding.

ROWELL: As I listen to your comments, I was reminded of Alice Walker's short story "1955."

MOTEN: Yes, she's definitely attuned to the secret and to the question of the secret, the problem of its marketing, and the racial limits of its comprehension. But her story also, it seems to me, demands that we consider—on the other side of sheer thievery and impossible imitation—someone like Bob Dylan maybe listening to The Mississippi Sheiks and Roscoe Holcomb doing very different performances of "Sittin' on Top of the World," the secret in blues and bluegrass, both versions of the secret crucial in Dylan's singular forging of his own. Dylan talks about what he calls Holcomb's "untamed sense of control" in ways that let you know, in apposition to Walker's formulations, that the secret is only transmitted in transformation and transmutation.

ROWELL: Are there cultural secrets in the two Brazilian art forms: samba, an African-Brazilian invention, and bossa nova, a European-Brazilian invention after samba. Were the whites attempting to possess the secrets of samba in their appropriation of that black form in their creation of bossa nova?

MOTEN: I don't know enough about bossa nova to make any kind of definitive claim though when I listen to João Gilberto (and then to Gilberto Gil's sort of devoted interruption of him) I hear something that might be thought of as much in terms of possession by samba as possession of samba. But I'm only beginning to listen to this beautiful music, to claim it, and let it make its claim on me. Browning writes very beautifully about samba, about the ways samba reveals that possession is also always being possessed and dispossessed, a loss of one's self-possession by holding and by being held by what it is you think to be your own. While attempting to stave off any naive romanticism regarding the salutary effects of racial mixture, especially given the brutal ways power can deploy it in the same interests for which it also deploys racial purity, it's still necessary to consider the potentially fruitful ways that whiteness is disturbed and blackness reconfigured by Gilberto in his context and Dylan in his. They both contribute to the international of beautiful and necessary obscurity.

ROWELL: From the angle of the maker or from the angle of the subject?

MOTEN: I think this secret that I'm talking about is both in the maker and the maker's subject. I listen to some music that I love and it inspires me to write a poem. My poem is not going to be that music. And if my poem only attempts to imitate that music, it's not going to be worth a lot. But if it's an attempt to get at what is essential to that music, perhaps it will approach the secret of the music, but only by way of that secret's poetic reproduction (some singular thing given in falling short or in going past but also in the intuition of and desire for the connection with the subject that prompted it). Derrida once said that "what is happily and tragically universal is absolute singularity": that's the secret—that the poem contains and is structured by the irreducible generality of human making and the political, economic, and erotic particularity of a given making. Art is the transmission of the secret, but the secret is transmuted in every moment of its transmission. I think that transmutation must show up as obscurity; but such obscurity must also be recognizable; an obscurity that people can feel and know, but not necessarily by way of supposedly simple and supposedly direct declarative statements.

ROWELL: I want to go back to your idea of poetry as a mode of inquiry. Whose mode of inquiry? Is it only that of the poet or maker, or is it also that of the reader? When you commit yourself as a reader to reading a poem, are you committing yourself to inquiring, or has the maker/poet already done that for you?

MOTEN: I would say that inquiry is transmitted and transmuted in the same way that the secret is. Inquiry is directed toward the secret but it is directed by the secret as well. At the same time, reading a poem is a mode of inquiry into a mode of inquiry; it is, hopefully, a response to a creative and questioning call that is also creative and questioning. Such reading is best characterized by the word "generosity." Writing, reading, or teaching art is like passing the gift of some inexhaustible disruption from hand to hand. You mess with it and it messes with you. This is a question concerning love and politics but see, that formulation is too "simple" and too "direct"; now I'm just babbling.

ROWELL: You have already spoken a lot about music, but I will still ask this question or make these comments about music and your own work. One of the most unmistakable features of your poetry is its grounding in musical traditions as well as in twentieth-century American poetic traditions. Will you talk about the importance of these two groups of traditions to you as a poet? I am not talking about the contents of your poems so much as I am speaking of the art or the craft or the making of your poems.

MOTEN: Although there is a whole set of very complicated, well-developed, and well-defined protocols within which music is created and received, music is not constrained by the requirement to mean in the way that language is so constrained. It is in this sense, according to Louis Zukofsky, Baraka, Harryette Mullen, and a whole bunch of others, that music becomes a limit that poets attempt to approach. But even though music is not constrained by meaning, no one would ever say that music doesn't bear content or that music doesn't have something to say. So I'm trying to write poems that are situated in relation to this question: how is it that a work can bear content, have something to say, while not being wholly bound to the constraints and the requirements of making meaning? At the same time, I never want totally to refuse either the requirement or opportunity that is given in poetry to produce meaning. I want to write poems that recognizably inhabit, but in some kind of underground or fugitive way, the space between the laws of music and the laws of meaning. I want to challenge the law that language lays down while taking advantage of the opportunity that language affords. Of course, with regard both to language and to music, the African Diaspora is a global experimental field in which the laws of valuation, phonic organization, and graphic (re)production are constantly placed under the severe pressure of questioning and creativity. In "Ev'rytime We Say Goodbye," Cole Porter writes: "There's no love song finer / but how strange, the change, / from major to minor"; but what Betty Carter does both to these words and to that change takes Porter's composition out into the very economy, the very discovery, of the secret (of loss and of love) that he wished to transmit. She moves against the laws he broke and made, and I want to move on her line (which is also Baraka's line and Mullen's line, but also, by way of different protocols, different versions of the secret, Porter's line and, in a whole other way, on wholly other terrain, Zukofsky's line as well).

ROWELL: In your critical text, *In the Break*, you made a statement that I think informs your own poetry. You were speaking of Cecil Taylor's poem "Chinampas": "This loosening is part of Taylor's method: of the word from its meaning, of the wounds from the word in the interest of a generative reconstruction, as if all of a sudden one decided to refuse the abandonment of the full resources of language, as if one decided no longer to follow the determining, structuring, reductive force of law."

MOTEN: In Nathaniel Mackey's great essay "Cante Moro," he discusses—by way of Federico Garcia Lorca's elaboration of the term "duende" as well as some amazing stuff Baraka has to say about how saxophonist John Tchicai's tone and phrasing "slide away from the proposed"—a particular quality of sound that implies and encodes movement, restlessness, a kind of fugal and centrifugal desire and execution that he calls "fugitivity." This sound is indicative of something that one is possessed by; it indicates, finally, life; that, as Foucault says, life constantly escapes; it steals away. Art works this way, too, I think; this sliding away from the proposed, this placement of the truth or of the secret in that space of tension or movement that is characterized by obscurity and indirection is what [Theodor] Adorno calls art's "immigrant law of motion." That law is given, and as its breaking, in a sound, in the dispossessive tension between music and meaning that Harryette Mullen talks about under the rubric of the "runaway tongue." This is the sound of the resistance to slavery; the critique of (private) property and of the proper, and it is, in the radical transformationality of all of its reproduction and recording, its commodified dissemination and circulation, irreducible and ongoing. That sound infuses Taylor's art and that's what I was trying to get at in the passage you quote. He's operating on a plane (and in a plain) of desire in which freedom and justice, each in its own complicated relation to law, are envisioned as unopposed to one another. That's our tradition. It is fugitive, even criminal, but not lawless. It is, as musician and musicologist Salim Washington says, a tradition of freedom but not of license. It's not but nothing other than the tradition within which Holcomb exerts his "untamed sense of control." I can't help thinking of a vast set of ranges and styles of fugitivity: Mondrian's and Shakespeare's (and now I'm back to the question that precedes the one I'm supposed to be answering) and Rakim's and Aretha's. But, see, this is the trouble with talking about traditions and the qualities that inform them: you just start babbling and dropping names. In the end, that's probably all my writing is—dropping names and droppin' things, like Betty Carter.

ROWELL: Here at the beginning of the twenty-first century, I see our poets reading us into a variety of forms—texts like your own, those of Thomas Sayers Ellis, Natasha Trethewey, Carl Phillips, and so many others. Aesthetically, I view us as a long distance from the Black Arts Movement. And yet that is not to say that the poets of that movement do not have anything to offer us. Your poems and your critical texts tell me that the Black Arts Movement was an informing necessity in African-American expressive culture, and that it is an informing necessity in African-American culture, the same way the Harlem Renaissance must be. The same as such writers as Richard Wright, James Baldwin, and Ralph Ellison continue to be. Is there a relationship between the experimentalism of the Black Nationalist art and the foundations of aesthetics in African-American vernacular culture? Are that experimentalism and the aesthetic of vernacular culture important to your work? Oh, I did not mean to ask you so many questions at one time. [*Laughter.*]

MOTEN: But all those questions are part of the same question and that's cool because this problem of the one and the many characterizes the Black Arts Movement as well as what it is that the Black Arts Movement was trying to approach and to convey: the multiple oneness of blackness (like what Trinh T. Minh-Ha calls "the multiple oneness of life") in its relation to the history and hope of a radical political comportment; something inextricably bound to escape, fugitivity, criminality. So for me the Black Arts Movement is crucial and indispensable. And this is not only because of the range and depth of its address—however complicated and problematic—of fundamental questions but also because it was under that movement's protocols and emphases that I was introduced to art. My mom was a teacher and I remember going to work with her during Black History Week in the late sixties when I was five or six, watching and sometimes participating in the little programs and presentations in which she would direct her third- and fourth-grade students. One time she had the kids doing some kind of performance, the music for which was a song by the Temptations called "Message to the Black Man" from an album called Puzzle People. The refrain from that song—"No matter how hard they try they can't stop us now" was imprinted on my brain. I can hear it right now in what feels like the same way that I first heard it. Anyway, the point is that that song and my mom's adaptation and contextualization of it were all operating under the umbrella, so to speak, of the Black Arts Movement. That movement, that cultural field, was formative for me and, I think, for a lot of other scholars and poets of my generation. My mom had Baraka's and Larry Neal's anthology Black Fire and another anthology edited by Abraham Chapman called Black Voices; I remember her talking to me when I was very small about the beauty of George Jackson's writing in Soledad Brother. These books are still on my shelves, held together by rubber bands. In Black Voices there's a poem by Mari Evans called "Black Jam for Dr. Negro," whose sound will never leave my head. I knew that stuff before I knew Chaucer or Milton; it remains formative for me and beautiful. Now, that doesn't mean there aren't elements of the Black Arts Movement that require critique. I hope that *In the Break* adequately expresses both the depth of my love for that particular cultural formation, even in the moments when I'm trying to be critical of it in a rigorous and severe way. I'm talking now about the key figure in that movement and the one who's at the center of my book. Baraka is not only the condition of possibility of my writing but also almost always anticipates my critiques of him even though the critiques remain necessary. I'm thinking, particularly, of a set of questions concerning the sexual politics of the Black Arts Movement that converge with some questions regarding its racial politics as well as its relation to bohemianism and experimentalism. Baraka writes about both the loudness (which is to say both the publicness and the sharpness) of the changing of his ways and, more famously, of the sameness of what changes in black cultural life more generally. This is important when one considers that the participation in and delineation of the Black Arts by Baraka and others emerges by way of, as well as in response to, bohemian experimentation. Baraka's downtown New York sojourn is carried over into and enables the very formation that disavows it; but it is just as important to recognize that the presence of Baraka, A. B. Spellman, Robert Thompson, Archie Shepp, Cecil Taylor, Adrienne Kennedy, Adrian Piper, and Samuel R. Delany meant that the downtown thing was also always a black thing and, in certain complicated ways, also a Black Arts thing. Downtown was one of the points of transformation—if not origin—of Baraka's experiment. Baraka carries an experiment, a secret, with him that changes with him and by way of him. After he leaves downtown, Baraka carries the experiment to Harlem in a return that is not a return of the native who is not a native; and after a short stop he goes to Newark, carrying his version of the experiment back to where you could be fooled into thinking it started. The experiment/alism that he carries (back) to Newark vibrates with the radicalism of black everyday life and the energy of advanced American poetics (which was, itself, never not either seeking to own or to disavow itself as a black thing). I think there's a very intense relationship between experimentalism and the everyday (which includes but is not reducible to what people call "the vernacular") that animates radical artistic practice in the second half of the twentieth century generally and that the Black Arts Movement helped to conceptualize it. But that relation was already in place, it seems to me, in Zora Neale Hurston's work or Ma Rainey's. This is to say that stuff that gets placed under the rubric of the black vernacular is as much an experiment as that which is coded as avant-garde. I know I'm rambling, but so does the experiment in its necessary obscurity and promiscuity, in the freedom in constraint of a crawlspace or a middle passage.

ROWELL: The Black Arts Movement created a generation of African-American poets. Rita Dove and Yusef Komunyakaa represent another generation that comes after the Movement. Two more generations follow these two poets. How would you describe recent black poetry? Can we pin it down the way we can the poetry of the Movement? I am willing to celebrate the poetry being written now because it is not controlled by a collective or individual prescription or dictum. The poets are now as free as our jazz musicians; they are free to create out of themselves, their own private lives, which is the source of all art. The new poets are striking out in so many different directions and coming up with so much. I consider this to be an extraordinary time in African-American poetry. There is a lot happening.

MOTEN: That's very true and yet I think there was always a lot happening. The Harlem Renaissance was broad enough to contain the vast formal difference between Claude McKay and Langston Hughes just as the Black Arts Movement was expansive enough to encompass Sonia Sanchez and Haki Madhubuti. And when you consider that at the same time you've got Gwendolyn Brooks and Robert Hayden, N. H. Pritchard and Julia Fields, it makes you kind of wonder, on the one hand, how folks could blind themselves to such diversity and, on the other hand, how others could take such blindness so seriously. Anyway, the point is that now there is a whole bunch of great black poets writing, performing, and recording in a whole bunch of ways and that is extraordinarily exciting. Between Ed Roberson's architecture and Tracie Morris's acoustics and these old MC Lyte twelve-inches I've been playing I don't know what do with myself. It's too much! Obviously, there are significant differences both between these poets and between those types of poetry that foreground either the literary or the performative; nevertheless, you can't help but recognize the kinship between them and I just want to be part of the family.

Fred Moten is an associate professor of English at Duke University. He is
the author of *Hughson's Tavern* (Leon Works, 2008); *I ran from it but was
still in it* (Cusp Books, 2007); *In The Break: The Aesthetics of the Black
Radical Tradition* (Minnesota, 2003); with Jim Behrle, *Poems* (Pressed
Wafer, 2002); and *Arkansas* (Pressed Wafer, 2000).

Library of Congress Cataloging-in-Publication Data

Moten, Fred.
B Jenkins / Fred Moten.
p. cm.—(Refiguring American music)
"The interview printed at the end of this book originally appeared as "Words don't
go there : an interview with Fred Moten," Callaloo 27, no. 4 (2004): 953/66."
ISBN 978-0-8223-4684-5 (cloth : alk. paper)
ISBN 978-0-8223-4696-8 (pbk. : alk. paper)
I. Title.
II. Series: Refiguring American music.
PS3563.O8867B54 2010
811'.6—dc22
2009037183

38902572R00076